How To Manage Your Money

There Is A Comprehensive Guide That Will Teach You
How To Effectively Manage Your Money And Improve
Your Lifestyle

*(Learn How To Handle Your Finances So That You Can
Easily Accumulate Wealth And Retire Earlier)*

Michel Rieger

TABLE OF CONTNET

How to Make a Budget

If you don't have enough money to do all you want, this planning approach might help you prioritise your spending and focus your money on the things that matter most to you.

Why is budgeting so important?

By creating a spending plan with a budget, you can ensure that you always have enough money for the things you need and those that are essential to you. You can keep out of debt or, if you are currently in debt, help yourself out of it by sticking to a budget or spending plan.

Start creating a budget.

Budgeting is the best method to take charge of your finances and ensure that your money is spent on the things that are most important to you, even though it can be challenging to create and stick to.

As you draft your customised budget, take the following actions:

Enumerate your basic principles. After determining your priorities, prioritise your values.

Establish some goals.

Write down your goals.

Think about your financial objectives for the next three years, years, and six months.

Decide on your revenue.

Determine your alternatives for income (your take-home or net salary).

Leave it out because overtime money shouldn't be your main source of revenue.

Decide on your expenses.

Examine your retail receipts, credit card statements, register, chequebook, and other documents.

Where does your money disappear to?

"Fixed expenses" like rent, car payments, and student loan instalments are easy to figure out.

Entertainment, clothes, and other "flexible expenses" have monthly variations in cost.

Don't forget to factor in taxes and insurance paid quarterly, semi-annually, or annually.

Consider using a budgeting tool in your personal finance programme to help you keep track of these expenses.

Make a spending plan.

Think of your budget as a "spending plan" that will assist you in monitoring your income, expenses, and surplus funds.

Prioritise your "needs" before any "wants" you can afford in your spending plan.

There should be a range of expenses that correspond to your whole income.

If your salary isn't enough to pay for everything, you should decide which expenses can be reduced to adjust your spending and budget.

Pay yourself first!

Saving is a crucial part of protecting your money.

Save as much as you can every month. Even a bit can make a big difference if you stick with it. Use our savings calculator to learn more.

Establishing an emergency savings account large enough to cover three to six months' worth of living expenses is a great idea.

Goals can be attained with savings once you have an emergency reserve.

When using credit cards, exercise caution.

Return often.

Keep a regular schedule for reviewing your finances.

Does the plan still help you achieve your objectives and fulfil your needs? If not, adjust or create a new budget that more closely aligns with your needs.

Chapter 3: CULTIVATING A LIFESTYLE ORIENTED IN SUCCESS

Success in life requires more than just good fortune or innate ability. Instead, it calls for a conscious effort to develop a lifestyle focused on success by embracing particular routines, attitudes, and actions consistent with achieving and sustaining success over time. It's similar to constructing a road to success, one step at a time, by establishing specific objectives and acting consistently to meet them. It all comes down to accepting that success is attainable and then putting forth deliberate effort to make it so.

The following are essential components of a lifestyle focused on success:

Establishing Objectives: The key to success is establishing specific and measurable objectives. It all comes down to figuring out what you want to accomplish and planning to get there. Establishing and maintaining short.

Lifelong Learning: People who achieve success are lifelong learners. They know how crucial it is to always be learning new things to change conditions. You may continuously advance towards your goals and develop yourself by actively seeking learning opportunities, such as reading books, attending workshops or courses, and asking peers or mentors for comments.

Productivity and Time Management: Success requires both productive and effective time management. It's about setting priorities, controlling outside distractions, and optimising your time. You can increase productivity and move closer to your objectives by developing a routine or plan, dividing work into digestible portions, and using productivity tools.

Resilience and Perseverance: Failures are unavoidable, and achieving success is not always easy. To overcome obstacles and keep going forward, it is essential to cultivate resilience and tenacity. It's about overcoming setbacks, remaining dedicated to your objectives, and persevering through difficult times.

Good Work-Life Harmony: A healthy work-life balance is essential for long-term success. It's about ensuring that you have the stamina. Setting limits between your personal and professional lives, putting self-care first, and spending quality time with your loved ones are all ways to keep your lifestyle balanced and satisfying.

Networking and Relationship Building: Success depends on developing a solid network and enduring partnerships. Having a supportive and like-minded group of people around you can give you access to chances, resources, and insightful people who can help you succeed. Building professional relationships, attending industry events, and actively networking can all help you grow your network and discover new prospects.

Above all, developing a success-oriented lifestyle necessitates a mentality shift that includes modifying your pessimistic attitudes, convictions, and practices towards finances, employment, and lifestyle. The following significant mental adjustments can assist you in escaping the rat race:

Financial mindset: It's critical to change your perspective from living paycheck to paycheck to creating wealth and financial abundance. This includes realising the value of investing, saving, and prudent money management. It also entails changing your perspective from materialism and consumerism to purposeful spending and accumulating assets that yield passive income.

Growth-oriented thinking Developing a growth mentality, which prioritises ongoing education, self-improvement, and prudent risk-taking, can assist you in escaping the never-ending treadmill. This entails having an open mind, learning new things, and always looking for methods to advance and develop personally and professionally.

Entrepreneurial attitude: Developing an entrepreneurial mindset can help you escape the never-ending cycle of work and play. This entails adopting an innovative, creative, and risk-taking mindset and being open to investigating and pursuing business endeavours that may offer increased freedom, flexibility, and the possibility to build money.

Breaking free from the rat race may also require changing your perspective from trading time for money to valuing your time and lifestyle. Developing a life that aligns with your values and aspirations entails setting aside time for pursuits that make you happy and fulfilled and lead to a balanced existence.

The mindset of possibilities and abundance: Changing your perspective from one of possibilities and scarcity to one of abundance will help you escape the rat race. This includes the conviction that you are surrounded by plenty of opportunity and that, with enough effort, wise decisions, and persistence, you can design the life you want.

A mental change is necessary to escape the rat race; this includes altering your attitudes, beliefs, and actions towards opportunities, money, employment, and lifestyle. By developing an optimistic and empowering mindset, you can move towards financial independence and a more contented, self-sufficient life.

The Reasons Behind Investing in Financial Education

Try Ignorance If You Think Investing Education Is Expensive.

Could you distinguish between an income statement and a balance sheet?

Do you know the necessary measures for conducting due diligence before risking money on a new investment?

Do you know the distinctions between gambling and saving and how they impact your earnings?

Surprisingly, schooling does not impart the most important skill that can make or break your financial success. After completing your four years of study, you will have little investment or personal money knowledge.

Physicians and solicitors will begin practising without knowing how to interpret a financial statement. Investors and business owners may continue to be dangerously uninformed about tax laws.

Financial literacy is the most important skill you need to acquire to accumulate wealth and experience financial security. There isn't a substitute.

Investing in financial education is one of the best things you can do for yourself. It's the beginning of building wealth. One thing to remember is that you can earn a four-year degree yet have little knowledge of personal finance. You could start a company even though you're unfamiliar with financial statements.

Thus, acquiring financial literacy requires a substantial commitment. Here are five explanations for this:

The greatest investment you can make is in yourself and your financial literacy. The obvious place to start when building money is here.

These are the causes:

• Boosts your productivity and offers everlasting profits that no one can ever take away from you.

• Boosts the return on your investment.

• Enhances your life and stable financial situation.

• Make sure your withdrawal is secure.

• Provides investors with protection against unnecessary loss; • Offers people peace of mind.

The list of pros is lengthy, but what are the drawbacks? Why is it that not everyone acquires the skills required to invest and raise their level of financial literacy?

There are no other negatives other than the requirement for time and effort. You may gain all the advantages of becoming financially literate if you are prepared to put in the necessary time. All you need to do to claim a lifetime of benefits is put in some effort.

It's one of those "obvious" choices that are simple to understand yet challenging to implement.

In the end, which would you prefer—a lifetime of financial stability in exchange for a little commitment or a lifetime of financial mediocrity in exchange for a little disruption and avoidance now?

It's not a difficult choice, but relatively few people choose wisely.

Financial education is one of the best investments you can make since it has no costs, losses, or huge returns. You cannot find a better investment than this one.

It will be more crucial the quicker you obtain it. You will be more expensive the longer you wait. Which way will you decide to go?

To give you a better idea, we'll go over each of the seven reasons below why financial education is the best investment you can make.

1. The majority of investment advice is dangerously incomplete.

Are you not tired of the investment advice that contradicts itself, as provided by political and investment experts?

• Diversification reduces risk, according to one expert, while it increases risk and yields mediocre outcomes, according to another expert.

• Some experts argue that paying off all of your debt is a terrible idea, while others believe that some debt can be a beneficial way to build wealth.

• While some experts believe that the stock market is essential for prosperity, others believe real estate is the primary source of millionaires.

If so-called experts cannot agree, how does one learn to invest? Enough to get you moving! With whom can you have confidence? With whom can you have confidence?

Although every financial expert offers a unique and perhaps contradictory piece of investing advice, that authority speaks as though there is just one answer. It is not logical! It's stressful right now. It's stressful right now.

When financial analysts are said to speak in highly dogmatic and basic terms, as though they had the answer, it drives me nuts.

Experts understand that most financial realities are more subtle and intricate, so they won't insult your intelligence by oversimplifying sage investment advice.

Over time, even the most basic investment concepts—such as purchasing and keeping stocks—become too complicated for a media soundbite or brief piece to fully convey.

Ironically, the aforementioned contradicting investing advice problems are only partially accurate or false, depending on the circumstances.

It makes sense to take on new debt frequently, and it also makes sense to pay off bad debt occasionally.

"Buying and holding long-term stocks" is generally a wise course of action; however, occasionally, the risk is greater than the return.

Everybody is a dishonest half-truth. Thinking about the subtle shades of grey beneath all the half-truths you hear about investments is one way to support financial education.

How can you use this information to make profitable investing choices? Understanding conditional truths and when to ignore them is important since they might jeopardise you financially.

Do you know, for instance, when to buy and hold onto a wise investing strategy and when the potential return does not outweigh the potential risk?

Do you know when it makes sense to repay debt and when it should be used to raise capital?

Which is the most effective means of generating wealth: real estate, businesses, or paper properties? Why?

These kinds of questions will either make or break the financial future.

One justification for the necessity of financial education is the ability to comprehend the premises and rationale of the investing half-truths. This is the only way to sort through the convoluted and contradictory world of investment advice and determine who is right and wrong and why.

CHAPTER 4: MAKING DECISIONS

Making decisions is a talent that affects your experiences, opportunities, and personal development. It also determines the direction of your life.

"By developing your ability to make wise and practical decisions, you've given yourself a compass to help you navigate the challenges of life."

How Do You Make Decisions?

Consider life as a wide ocean, with your choices as the sails guiding your vessel. Making decisions involves weighing your options and choosing the best fit for your objectives, values, and situation. You have to make several daily decisions that affect your major and minor path. Making decisions that move you closer to your goals requires careful thought, balancing advantages and disadvantages, and making well-considered decisions.

How to Come to Wise Decisions

1. Compile Information: The Basis for Decision-Making Obtain pertinent data before judging. Do your homework, consult with experts, and weigh the possible outcomes of each choice. Consider each extracurricular activity's advantages, time obligations, and individual interests before committing.

2. Establish Your Priorities - The North Star of Choice: Make sure your priorities and values are clear. Making decisions consistent with your values is easier when you know what matters most to you. You might pick healthy meals over quick food if you value your health.

3. Examine Other Options - Broadening Your Views: Take your time making decisions. Investigate several choices, even if they don't seem traditional. This broadens your viewpoint and enables you to make a more well-rounded decision.

4. Assess Consequences - Predicting the Ripple Effect: Consider the possible results of every choice you make. Think about the long- and

short-term effects. Consider the effects of potential part-time work on your academic performance, social life, and general well-being.

5. Trust Your Instincts - Honour Your Gut Feeling: Occasionally, your intuition might offer insightful information. Even when logic tells you otherwise, if a choice seems right in your heart, it may be worthwhile to think it out.

6. Seek Advice - The Power of Collective Wisdom: Don't be embarrassed to consult mentors, family members, or trustworthy friends for advice. Their experiences can provide insightful viewpoints that affect your decision.

7. Exercise Patience - The Art of Timing: A period of introspection may benefit some judgements. Allow yourself enough time to reflect, go to bed, and return to the choice in a new light.

WHICH TYPE OF MINDSET ARE YOU?

Many business owners and entrepreneurs began as employees. They were employed by someone else. The problem is that breaking free from the worker attitude could be challenging if you have been employed for a considerable amount of time.

What does this mean, exactly?

If you have a representative mindset, you will seek other people to listen to you briefly. It will be difficult for you to accept responsibility for the success or failure of your endeavour.

As a representative, you don't influence how the business is run. All you do is try to prove yourself useful so that you may continue to be employed.

Which One Do You Own?

If you're an entrepreneur or business person, you think in novel ways about various things. In essence, it's you who stops (and starts) the game. You are responsible for the success or failure of your project. Furthermore, you make enormous decisions (including who gets to make the smaller ones!).

Take this short quiz to see if you think more like a worker or a businessperson:

• Do you limit your projects and responsibilities to a portion of what is necessary for your company's success?

• Do you balance your lifestyle with your income?

• When financial difficulties arise, do you modify your spending plan to account for the drop in income?

• Do you constantly seek advice from others to make decisions, even daily?

You most likely have a worker mindset if you answered "yes" to most of these questions. This is why people with a business-minded perspective would say "no."

Do you limit your projects or responsibilities to a portion?

What is necessary for the success of your business? Businesspeople understand that there are times when they have tasks in their firm that are "above" or "below" their skill level. They're not opposed to rolling up their sleeves and getting their hands filthy, but their mental attitude may need to be developed.

Do you arrange your lifestyle for your earnings?

When financial setbacks occur, visionaries in business will try to grow their company, diversify their product offerings, and increase their services. They refuse to let their financial circumstances become or remain a victim of them.

In the unlikely event of a financial setback, do you reduce your spending to account for the drop in income? People in business usually send their instalments first. They concentrate on earning the necessary money to maintain their lifestyle and invest the remainder in their company. They share an understanding of and acceptance of the transient sacrifices necessary to achieve a goal. Do you constantly seek outside advice when making decisions, even daily?

People in business manage their time and take responsibility for their actions. They are in charge of their daily activities and don't require someone else to tell them what to do or prod them to do it, even though they may look for coaches to guide them towards longer development.

Chapter 4: Handling Debt

Debt can be a helpful instrument when reaching financial objectives like home ownership or school funding. It can, however, also turn into a burden if improperly handled. This chapter will cover debt management and reduction techniques.

Recognising Your Debt

To effectively manage your debt, you must first ascertain what you owe and to whom. List all your bills, such as mortgages, credit card balances, auto loans, and school loans. Note each debt's interest rate, minimum payment amount, and due date.

It's also critical to comprehend your credit score, a figure that indicates how creditworthy you are. It may be simpler to say your credit score is higher. Every year, Equifax, Experian, and TransUnion—the three main credit bureaus—offer free credit score checks.

Making a Plan to Pay Off Debt

You can make a debt payback plan after you have a thorough understanding of your obligations. Several debt repayment techniques exist, such as the avalanche and snowball methods.

Regardless of interest rate, the snowball method entails paying off debts from smallest to largest. Because you can see results quickly, this technique can provide you with a psychological lift, but it might not be the most economical in terms of interest paid.

Paying down debts in order of greatest to the lowest interest rate is known as the avalanche approach. Long-term interest cost savings are possible with this method, although results might take longer.

Regardless of the approach you take, it's critical to create and adhere to a budget. Look for places to save costs, including cutting back on eating out or terminating subscription services.

Taking Care of Credit Cards

While using credit cards to make purchases and establish credit can be handy, improper use can result in significant debt.

The following are some methods for handling credit cards:

• To avoid paying interest, pay off your entire total each month.

Avoid opening multiple credit cards simultaneously, which can lower your credit score. Search for cards with rewards programmes and cheap interest rates that fit your spending patterns. Keep your credit utilisation ratio low by not using more than 30% of your available credit.

How to Handle Debt Collectors

Debt collectors may contact you by phone or letter if you are behind on your payments. Being aware of your rights and acting professionally while interacting with debt collectors is critical.

Debt collectors are obligated by the Fair Debt Collection Practices Act to furnish specific information and abstain from coercive or intimidating methods.

Speak with a credit counsellor or a bankruptcy attorney if you are having trouble making debt payments. These experts may be able to negotiate on your behalf with creditors and offer advice on debt management.

In summary

An essential component of personal finance is debt management. You may take charge of your financial condition and strive towards becoming debt-free by being aware of your obligations, making a repayment plan, and controlling credit cards. Don't forget to create a budget, follow your plan, and, if necessary, acquire expert assistance.

Ensure Better Storage of Your Items

I'm always in awe of how people handle their possessions these days. People just don't seem to love their possessions enough to take care of and preserve them, whether it be their home, car, clothes, cell phone, or anything else that can be purchased.

I believe you will discover that over time, you will spend less money if you dedicate yourself to maintaining your belongings and trying your hardest to extend your lifespan.

If you own a car, for example, it is far better to maintain your vehicle regularly and replace the oil rather than pay a large sum when it breaks down.

It's simpler to keep things clean than to make them clean, as my dad used to say.

And, surprise! It's also less expensive!

3.

Eliminate Debt

Paying off debt should be your priority if you're trying to find strategies to lower your living expenses and pay monthly payments on any debt.

Although it's among the hardest things on this list, this is the finest approach to improving your financial situation.

Bringing Your Federal Student Loans Together

Your budget is heavily impacted by the $675 payment associated with the usual ten-year repayment plan, which is part of your $60,000 student loan debt. You'll soon have to decide which bills to prioritise: rent or college loans.

You are considering taking out a single loan with an extended repayment schedule. Even if your over $600 student loan payment weighs you down, you don't feel any better about having to continue making payments thirty years from now.

Alternatively, since lenders gave a veritable treasure of student loan savings before October 2007 (this book is for loans and borrowers of all ages), you did consolidate your debts. After thirty-six on-time payments, you obtained a two per cent interest rate reduction. However, you fear that you may lose your benefits if you experience a temporary inability to make payments due to a wage reduction.

Alternatively, let's say that you are a government worker who consolidated your loans after October 2007 and would like to reconsider them to direct lending to be eligible for loan forgiveness for public service after ten years.

Alternatively, you wish to add student loans from your time returning to school for an advanced degree, such as a master's, a Ph.D., or a law degree, so you are reconsolidating your student loans.

Alternatively, perhaps you consolidated within the previous few years and are wondering what to do if you lose your job and are momentarily unable to make payments or if another bank acquires your consolidation loan.

Whichever of these scenarios most closely matches your circumstances, there is a straightforward fix that only requires a few short actions and an examination of your unique financial situation. Strong warning: you might want to wait if you're reading this book before July 2024 and haven't consolidated your loans yet. Consolidation won't impact your payments towards forgiveness in late 2023. It might occur between June 30, 2024, and January 1, 2024.

If you are on an income-driven plan, starting in July 2024, consolidation of your student loans will not impact your payment count towards forgiveness. Additionally, payments from certain forbearance or deferment periods are being adjusted by the Department of Education to count towards income-driven payment counts. Hold off if you suspect you might be using income-driven payment choices. If you have previously consolidated, you can select the SAVE plan or another income-driven option. Continue reading in Chapter 2.

Define Consolidation.

Consolidation of federal student loans refers to taking all or part of your current federal student loans into a single new loan through one of your current services or direct lenders. One lender may provide all of the loans, or multiple lenders may provide them.

This is frequently done so that you only have to make one easy payment instead of having to plan payments for various loans from different semesters. Consolidation can also be done to incorporate new student loans, obtain a fixed interest rate, and obtain extra alternatives for repayment that are only available to direct lending loan borrowers.

Is It Time to Consolidate Your Debt?

Suppose you are unsure about whether to combine your loans. In that case, it is probably because you are unsure about which is more difficult to manage: making a larger payment now or paying more interest on your loans over a longer period. For instance, paying out

$60,000 in student loans over 30 years at the same interest rate would cost you $44,684 in interest, totalling $104,684; however, paying off $60,000 in student debt over 10 years at a 4.125 per cent interest rate would cost you $13,325 in interest, for a total of $73,325. Interest on a 30-year loan is $31,359 more. It would seem that you should continue on a ten-year plan as long as you can make your payments. Nonetheless, consolidating debt makes sense for the majority of borrowers.

Why?

You can repay your loans sooner when you consolidate them, but your payback period will be longer. You can even choose to pay it off in full after ten years. If you need it, you have a manageable payment in the interim that can be less than half of what would be needed throughout a ten-year payback plan. Furthermore, consolidation is your only option to obtain a fixed interest rate on any federal student loans with variable interest rates. What makes sticking to a ten-year plan desirable, then?

Continue if the normal ten-year payment plan enables you to maintain the discipline necessary to pay off your student loans in that amount of time. Just be sure you have the financial means to pay. But first, review the Personal Student Loan chart you made using the data you gathered from studentaid.gov in Chapter 1, "Evaluating Your Student Debt Situation." Consolidate your debts to obtain a guaranteed rate if your chart indicates that you have variable-rate loans.

You might think that making a smaller, aggregated payment will force you to continue making student loan payments for many years. In reality, though, it merely provides you with a payment you can always afford, with the option to increase it at any time.

PART TWO: SETTING FINANCIAL TARGETS

The first step towards financial stability and advancement is setting financial goals. Motivated and on track, regardless of your financial goals—saving for a big purchase, paying off debt, or saving for retirement. This is a clear method of stating your financial goals:

1. Determine Your Goals: Decide what you need to achieve financially before you start. These could be short-term goals like paying off credit card debt, medium-term goals like buying a house or travelling, or long-term goals like quitting easily.

2. Be Clear: Make sure your goals are as clear as possible. Instead of stating, "I need to save money," state, "I need to save $5,000 for an initial investment on a house in two years or less."

3. Establish a Schedule: Give each goal a reasonable time to complete. Understanding when you need to reach your goals can help you stay focused and create a savings plan.

4. Put Your Goals in Numbers: Link a specific financial amount to your goals. Knowing how much money you want to save for emergencies, invest, or cover advances can help you focus your efforts.

5. Set Prioritise Your Goals: Not all goals are created equal. Determine which are most important to you and give them special attention first. This ensures that your assets are distributed.

6. Make a spending plan: You'll need a financial strategy to reach your financial goals. Keep an eye on your earnings and expenses to identify where you might cut back and reallocate resources to your goals.

7. Track Progress: Regularly assess your financial goals and track your progress. This enables you to acknowledge your achievements and make adjustments as needed.

8. Remain flexible: Things might change financially, and life is unpredictable. When

circumstances change, be prepared to adjust your goals and plans.

Seek Expert Assistance: If your goals involve complicated financial matters, such as retirement planning or investing, you might want to consult a financial counsellor for guidance.

10. Exercise Restraint: It takes responsibility and discipline to reach financial goals. Follow your budget, avoid unnecessary expenses, and don't abandon your goals.

Knowing the fundamentals of investing

Investing is the process of giving your money a long-term purpose to increase its cash flow. It is comparable to sowing a seed with the hope that it will develop into a bigger plant. These are the foundations to help you understand investing simply.

1. Establishing Goals: Consider what you need to achieve before investing. Are you building wealth, buying a house, or saving for

retirement? Your investment approach will depend on your goals.

2. Return and Risk: Investing entails some risk. The possibility of larger returns usually accompanies higher risks. For example, stocks can yield enormous gains but carry greater risk than bonds or savings accounts. Assess your ability to withstand risk in light of your goals and your comfort level with possible highs and lows.

3. Diversification: Spread out your holdings across several locations. After that, the options are virtually limitless. Because other investments may increase in value if one declines, this can help reduce risk.

4. Time Skyline: It affects how long you want to be involved. You can brave market fluctuations when you have longer time horizons. If you want to receive the money quickly, you could want additional short-term, safe investments.

5. Expenses: Understand the expenses associated with your capital. Exorbitant fees eventually reduce your returns. Look for options with low expenses, like ETFs or record assets.

6. Research: Learn as much as possible about the investments you are considering. Look into the companies when buying stocks. Determine the goals and execution history of common assets, or ETFs.

7. Consistency: Investing in small amounts regularly, sometimes referred to as risk minimization, might be a wise strategy. In this sense, you spend less on high expenses and more on low costs.

8. Be patient: Investing isn't a hoax. It's a protracted match. In light of transient fluctuations in the market, exercise patience and refrain from making snap decisions.

9. Review and Adjust: Make sure your investments align with your goals by

periodically reviewing them. If your goals or situations change, adjust your portfolio.

10. Professional Advice: Seeking advice from a financial expert who can provide tailored guidance is a good idea if you're unsure about investing or are new to it.

Which would you favour more? Think back for a moment to your previous impressions on budgeting. Next, discard any unfavourable perceptions you may have about creating a budget. Your mind will be open to knowing more about it and how it can improve your life once you've completed it. You'll be able to justify yourself if you let your mind acclimatise to this new viewpoint.

1. EXCUSE: You desire autonomy. Reality: Those with a budget can plan their financial expenditures.

2. EXCUSE: What people think of you matters. REALITY: A budget allows you to make the most of your money on activities and material

possessions, enhancing your reputation for thrifty living.EXCUSE: You have no justification for doing so. Reality: There's no justification for devaluing your money.

Excuse: The concepts of personal finance can be dull. REALITY: These ideas can assist you by identifying what is preventing you from achieving your goals.

ACTION ITEM

There will be one action item in every chapter. If you would like, this section will walk you through looking into and using the information. The action item is as follows: Why, you might ask?

Every effective strategy starts with a purpose and concludes with an adaptable structure. Reversing this order is never appropriate. The two most crucial resources for reaching your objectives are time and money. Your why will become clear to you, so you should take the time to understand how to create a budget.

Budgeting turns out to be the most stylish attendee at the party, as you will quickly learn.

Thus, ask yourself: What is your main objective? To pay off debt, increase your awareness of your finances, save for a trip, pay off debt, or plan for retirement. These are all typical justifications for making a budget. It won't matter if you can create a convincing "why" of your own.

Think about your objective rather than focusing on how bad your budgeting is. Next, consider your objective and make a budget. After considering it, go on to the following chapter and consider why you need a budget.

Conditioning

Here are a few things that you may have mentioned. Making a budget takes time and effort. Keeping an eye on my expenditures is not enjoyable. Too much work goes into keeping track of my spending. While these remarks may be accurate, they are frequently uttered by those who haven't given them any thought. Everybody is a creature of habit. Whether we know it or not, our actions unconsciously programme our ideas and behaviours.

The psychologist B.F. Skinner is credited with coining the phrase operant conditioning. Behavioural psychologists use this word to characterise learning strategies that incorporate incentives or penalties. Behaviour can be produced by combining positive reinforcement and negative consequences, as shown by Skinner's research.

In society, people are encouraged to accept specific behaviours through positive reinforcement (to a certain culture). The application of negative reinforcement curbs unacceptable behaviour. Over time, each of us forms patterns that shape our behaviour. Conditioning shapes our beliefs; it is the familiar environments and standards we are exposed to. Our consciousness is shaped by our upbringing, whether we realise it or not.

Operant training frequently goes undercover as "rules." It is these unconscious patterns that shape our actions. Frequently, programmes are what start these patterns. Analyse your initial response to the following inquiries:

Have you ever made a plan before?

How frequently do you assess your development?

Negatively reacting people are probably not very hard workers. Or they think trying would be too tough. Maybe hate or fear of failing caused it? Is it possible that some training unintentionally conditioned an unconscious reaction?

You might have a bad attitude about money management if you respond negatively to those questions. Being unable to set a budget or not enjoying it is not a reason for shame. You will discover a few helpful tools as you finish this workbook. You can utilise these tools to formulate a fresh response. After that, you can develop fresh, conditioned reactions to the stimuli. New habits will arise from this.

Determining Practical Goals.

A personal trainer can develop a bodybuilding regimen to assist in achieving their unique performance goals. In a similar spirit, well-considered financial objectives support creating an individual's plan for reaching them.

First and foremost, financial goals should be sufficiently described to influence financial behaviours.

For example, making a goal to pay off a $20,000 credit card debt in a year may motivate you to restrict your expenditures to material goods. Therefore, if you were offered the opportunity to make a costly credit purchase, you would say no.

You might be motivated if you set a two-year goal to quadruple your income.

Individual principles.

Basing your goals on these results will increase the likelihood that you will reach them because they will genuinely fulfil you throughout the entire process.

Furthermore, when you move up the financial ladder you have created for yourself instead of importing it from your partner, friends, neighbours, or relatives, The amount of money you have saved and the number of ambitions you have realised determine your level of success.

Developing a keen awareness of your values, health, way of life, relationships, career, education, and the welfare of all people is an excellent concept.

Do you value volunteering in your community, spending time with your family, and keeping things simple? Ambitions and self-awareness may overshadow your enjoyment.

Suppose you prioritise your beliefs and set your income objectives based on what you consider non-negotiable. In that case, you will have a better chance of meeting your needs inside and outside your growing financial situation.

Realistic Budgetary Objectives.

A healthy dose of realism is also necessary to overcome subconscious goal-setting. If left to its own devices, a subconscious target and financial pattern will aim for a sum of money so unrealistic that no viable plan for advancement can be developed.

Even worse, the person becomes stuck in a dysfunctional cycle as a result of the subsequent inaction, which serves to reinforce the emotional theme of deprivation. Reducing the likelihood of anything like this occurring and advancing a practical action plan are realistic objectives.

You might be able to benefit from options like working with a professional or negotiating lower credit card interest rates just by admitting that you have debt. You can accept a part-time job to get a little extra money. If you genuinely desire to reduce your debt and have a set of realistic goals in place, nothing may stand in your way. This also applies to increasing your income, savings, assets, or capacity to purchase a new home. This steady movement yields more comfort and maybe longer-lasting results than chasing after unrealistically large wealth bubbles.

1. Examine your morals.

Consider the likelihood that you will create goals that you can achieve. Write each one down in your prosperity diary, beginning with a sentence such as this: • It is essential to me to spend time with my kids at least once a day; • It is essential that my employer values my abilities and my success as a business owner; • It is essential to me to have health insurance at my place of employment. For me, locating a steady stream of residual money is essential.

I place high importance on connections with my partner, spouse, and kids, as well as honesty, compassion, dependability, and privacy. I value having a peaceful place of employment, getting paid fairly for my work, and having a good relationship with my place of worship, religion, and a higher power. From the list you have created, select five unachievable claims. Consider the statements as representations of your guiding beliefs, which you will always honour regardless of how difficult things may appear.

2. Establish Long-Term Goals.

Create a form that looks like the one below, and in the right-hand column, write your goals for the next five to 10 years. This form distinguishes between net worth and yearly income.

It considers your available funds, the valuation of your belongings, debt, and desired net worth in greater detail. To become a billionaire, you need to have a million dollars in net worth rather than income.

Investing, debt repayment, accumulating more money, or purchasing pricey items can all be equated to net worth.

3. Select short-term lifestyle objectives. Determine shorter-term benchmarks based on your responses to the following questions to move closer to your long-term goals: What actions should I take to fulfil my long-term non-financial goals? Which objectives will I dedicate my attention to for the next three months? Which of these will I dedicate myself to in the upcoming year?

4. Establish annual financial goals. Set measurable one-year goals that support your long-term financial targets for income and net worth to achieve success.

After each year, revise these objectives as needed. For example, your one-year objective might be to double your net worth if your long-term target is to double it in seven years; over the next six years, you should seek to increase the percentage of gain each time. Include specific tactics in your one-year financial goals to increase your income and net worth. Increasing business earnings, paying higher salaries, and making investments with higher yields are all possible means of boosting income.

5. Promote and evaluate your financial goals.

Suppose that you have already attained your financial objective. Suppose you have $50. You decide to look into investing opportunities as you weigh your possibilities for further funding. Update your goals along the way, changing any incorrect information.

After that, practise making investments. Select a stock and begin "paper trading," deciding how many shares to buy at what price, keeping an eye on it, and eventually deciding when to sell it.

Consider purchasing a few stocks once your gains have exceeded your losses.

Examining houses within a certain budget range can also be helpful.

What new furniture would I have to purchase? Does the neighbourhood meet my criteria for safety? What effect will it have on them that my kids are here? Depending on your answers to these questions, you might need to reassess your goals for your lifestyle.

6. Typical methods of making money.

Include exchanging your time for money through employment or a service-oriented business, purchasing and reselling products for a profit, and creating passive income sources like rental property income and book investments.

Raise your status in the company or get a better position elsewhere. Alternatively, you could create residual income or acquire and sell goods to augment your income from work. WhicheveWhatevery you decide on, it support you in achieving your lifestyle objectives and aligns with your values. Once you plan, note any new knowledge or abilities you must use.

7. Visualise accomplishing your goals. You can become more open to new opportunities. The

most effective visualisations have both connected feelings and mental imagery.

• Take a seat in a chair with your hands gently resting on your lap and your legs flat on the ground or crossed at the ankles. To help you focus, take a few deep breaths. As you inhale and exhale, pay attention to your chest and abdomen. If your mind is active, keep breathing deeply and simply observe it without making any judgements.

If your mind is busy, observe it without making any judgements. Once you are relaxed, let your breathing return to normal and imagine yourself reaching a long-term goal related to your finances or lifestyle. Picture yourself in this state of mastery, enjoying your successes and bringing others joy, happiness, or pride. Take some time to linger with this idea and feeling. After that, silently say your affirmations, like "I've reached my goal" or "I live in the house of my dreams," without opening your mouth. Keep picturing the sensation of reaching your goal and the desired emotional states.

You can make any additions to the picture to better visualise the people you want to show the final product to. Refocus your attention whenever it strays.

Chapter 3: Creative Ways to Reduce Expenses

◆◆◆

Overview

For some, cutting expenses is not an easy task. But this is essential, particularly for those who don't want to be short on cash over the next few weeks. Cutting costs can be accomplished by thinking of creative ideas that are great for everyone, regardless of their financial situation or choice of school.

You can look at several options to cut costs while you're learning. Here are a few original concepts you might want to think about:

Making a budget could help you reduce your expenditures. Not only can you record your weekly or daily expenses using this, but you can also see which expenses you can eliminate.

Creative Methods for Cutting Your Studying Expenses.

There's a great way to make a budget if you don't know how to plan one. Knowing your budget should be your priority. Next, enumerate your daily expenses. Setting a daily spending limit for yourself is a great idea. Additionally, this will prevent you from buying goods you wouldn't normally buy. After creating your budget, you could save a significant amount of money.

Just buy what you need to get.

Another great way to cut costs is to just buy what you need. Consider if the purchase is a need or a desire before making it. Once you've determined that it's a desire, let it go. Purchase only what you require to reduce costs.

Buying Smart Books.

Textbooks are very important to your research. However, reducing your spending does not mean you should stop buying books. You can buy the textbooks you need. However, look for other retailers who will reduce the cost of your valuable books or offer discounts. This will allow you to spend less money because you will get textbooks that are just as good as much more expensive ones.

Make use of exclusive deals.

There's also a great chance for students to save money. You may receive discounts from certain businesses or stores. Even while some stores provide 10% or less discounts, this is still a major problem, especially if you're trying to save money. If you prefer to purchase online, several websites could save you money. Searching for them on Google is the only thing you should do. You can find these discounts on some websites if you're unsure which is reliable.

Control Your Transportation Expenses.

In terms of transportation, you do not need to own a car or any particular kind of vehicle for regular travel. If your parents give you one, though, you might use it once in a while. Petrol prices might be high. But if there are any reductions, you always take advantage of them. You can use a bike instead of driving a car if you own a bike. By doing this, you can eliminate traffic and save money on petrol. Walking could be a great alternative if you live close to your university. This could also be the perfect kind of exercise.

Either prepare your food or buy inexpensive food.

Purchasing products from restaurants might sometimes increase your costs, allowing you to exceed your budget. Thus, prepare meals or buy cheap ones if at all possible. You may eat healthful meals and save money by doing this. Having access to culinary meals in your dorm or wherever you are staying can also help you get better at cooking.

There are several things you may do to lower your expenses. Take this seriously and stick to your planned spending plan to succeed. It might make a difference.

THE IMPACT OF STRUCTURED ORGANISATION

There are definite benefits to coordination. A few studies point to disruption as one of the main causes of people's negative experiences with anxiety at work and home. People begin to feel as though they can't work and that it's inappropriate for them—for their jobs or personal lives—when they are overly busy. You'll reap these many benefits as you grow more well-adjusted and live better.

You'll Have More Concentration

Focusing on a task that needs to be done is always more pleasant when you are organised since it allows you to take stock of your situation. Nobody is very adept at doing different jobs. Research has repeatedly shown that people just think they're very good at things, even though no one is.

You'll Increase Your Productivity

You will become extremely valuable when you organise, plan, and systematise every aspect of your life. Because so many people don't plan or coordinate in a way that makes them more useful, you will do more than the large majority.

Over Time, Your Power Will Increase

Even if you and everyone else have the same number of hours in a day, how you choose to spend that time will greatly benefit you. Because of the association of the time you have, you will feel you have more time even though you don't. For example, you're less likely to have to hang around aimlessly returning if you take a shopping list to the store.

There Will Be Less Stress for You

Your current situation, both at home and at work, will be less messy, which will relieve some of your burden. The main reason is that you avoid time wasters by not looking for stuff.

There Will Be Greater Work-Life Balance for You

It's not hard to feel tired these days. The work hours for most occupations are no longer as rigid as they formerly were. To be honest, many jobs require you to be there, as is to be anticipated. That said, no one will be upset if you attend your child's ball game rather than work if you learn to be organised and outperform everyone else.

Your Ability to Set and Meet Goals Will Improve

Being coordinated helps you distinguish between things that are important and things that are not as important. This suggests you can set more meaningful goals since you understand what matters most. Additionally, you will genuinely wish to perform and make a greater move due to your alliance.

Every Day Will Feel More Positive for You

A fun thing happens when your life is organised; you just start to feel happy. The basic answer is that your veins are not under as much chemical pressure. Along with this, you begin to feel more productive in day-to-day activities. Everyone is satisfied with that.

You'll Be More Creative

The idea that organisation and association can foster creativity may initially seem counterintuitive, but it is true. If many things are always interfering with your mind, it is impossible for it to enter a creative state. You can succeed by making the most of your current situation by setting it up creatively.

You'll Be More Energised and Excited Every Day

You'll feel more enthusiasm and zest for life when you get up and realise you can overcome your day and feel accomplished. Now that you know you will win, you must manage the day.

You'll Have Greater Independence

If, as of right now, all you seem to be able to do is work with very little enjoyment in your life and then make plans to enhance your life, you will inevitably come across more opportunities. Time opportunity is amazing because, as soon as you realise you have it, you will also realise you have financial opportunity. That is a really powerful material. Imagine how special your mornings would be if you'd planned everything out the night before. Consider the difference in dinnertime if you have everything planned and organised. How fun will it be to spend a Sunday playing golf instead of doing laundry now that you've decided to rethink it? Even if your day seems different from this one, it will be simpler if you've made time to include association in every aspect of your life.

YOUR SAVINGS You can use your savings for everything from long-term goals to unforeseen expenses. Saving money for unforeseen expenses like taxes, a new computer, or all of this year's Christmas gifts may be incredibly comforting and relieve financial stress. Saving money for long-term objectives, such as a stress-free retirement, a trip to Paris, a new device you've had your eye on for a while, or a down payment for a house, can be exciting and inspiring.

Increasing your savings is like investing in your future. It takes self-control and planning to save money for tomorrow because you can't spend it today. The more money you set aside, the closer you are to creating a future you can mould. Naturally, no one can predict the future, and focusing only on the future might make the present less joyful. However, doing the opposite—living in the moment, not making plans for the future, and putting your financial security in the hands of other people, fate, or chance—is a risky move that you will come to regret when the future arrives and proves to be less than secure or prosperous.

Living without savings equates to being unable to dream and strive for your goals.

Consequently, you will have to take out a loan for any large purchase, which raises the cost of the item significantly because of the interest you would pay. It implies a lack of excitement or a sense of accomplishment from achieving a goal or resisting the need to make an impulsive purchase immediately on credit. Little or no savings also means you won't have enough money to support your needs once you stop earning an income, which means you won't be able to retire when you want to.

Without money, there is no safety net. And having that safety net is crucial if you want to reduce the possibility of losing even the things you need daily. The absence of a security net suggests that you might be unable to fix your washing machine should it break down unexpectedly. This implies that you may have to postpone the holiday your kids have anticipated all year if you lose your job. If you are unable to pay for emergency medical care, you may lose your life, your health, or even your mobility.

This is what a life with savings looks like right now:

Comfort in knowing that your well-funded emergency fund will enable you to handle unforeseen crises

A feeling of accomplishment as you accumulate money for a car fund so you may replace your vehicle rather than needing to take out a costly loan.

a sense of exhilaration knowing that you are making progress towards significant life goals and that each month gets you one step closer to each one

the awareness that your retirement savings contributions will allow you to live a comfortable retirement

The main concern isn't whether you're saving $500, $20, or $1 a month. Even if you don't think there's a benefit to putting $1 a month aside for a major goal, trust me when I say there is. Progress is progress. Even though it might not seem like much now, there will be many opportunities to expedite this process once you get going, whether it be additional cash on hand at the end of the month, a tax refund, or a bonus at work. Once you start, you'll discover other methods to increase your savings. If you don't begin, however, you won't have a specific savings account to deposit your bonus or tax return, save for when you can spend it.

Savings provide an unmatched lifestyle and emotional fulfilment beyond simply having extra cash in your bank account.

How to Promote Your Brand and Take the Lead in Chapter Four

People will always choose to purchase goods from the seller who excels in their industry, which may be your company. People will only ever be attracted to a company that ranks second or third. Granted, and I'm sure any business would like to think of itself as the finest, but the truth is that your business isn't the best in the market, objectively or statistically. Whether it's soft drinks, apparel, shoes, music, movies, books, or restraint chains, there's a reason why brand names are so popular everywhere. Simply put, people are willing to pay more for a brand name because they believe it is of higher quality, trustworthy, and offers the best value.

Being the industry leader brings with it trust, quality, and goodwill. Therefore, it can be said that your objective as an online seller is to establish your brand and grow your company into a market leader rather than sell products directly to customers. To be recognised as a leader, you must establish your brand and dominate your area. Once you are the leader, people will flock to you first and search for additional possibilities. Remember that your ultimate goal is to be the best leader in your sector. When circumstances are tough, as they are now, people flock towards leaders because they are unwilling to risk their money for a product that might be of poorer quality, even if the price is better.

Have you become a leader in your niche and achieved market dominance? You have to be seen to the crowd now. As previously mentioned, the name of your brand should reflect your values. Because it adds a personal touch, name recognition in your own right is crucial for dominating your niche. There are several ways to accomplish this, but making your identity known and visible online is among the most crucial. You can collaborate with other marketers—sometimes even with rivals. Although print advertising in magazines and newspapers is legal, it's not the best method to promote your online company. When handled well, your Facebook social media advertising strategy can significantly increase brand recognition by spreading the word. Even if they choose not to click on the link, when they repeatedly see your name on the websites they frequent, they unconsciously link your brand to a specific product.

An interesting strategy many internet marketers overlook is affiliate marketing, a very simple and successful form of advertising. If your affiliates receive payment for referring customers to your goods, they will be highly motivated to promote your brand wherever they can to earn that commission. Even while you might have to forfeit some of your earnings to pay back the affiliates, a well-executed affiliate marketing campaign usually results in your business gaining momentum, growing rapidly, and being well-known.

Therefore, your objective is to have your name linked to your product through advertising or any other means, but when a customer purchases a product you are offering, they should keep you in mind.

Make a name for yourself. You have to be known as the "go to" person in your niche. Authority figures should be immediately trusted, and advice should be heeded. Establishing oneself in this role may be done in various ways, some of the more popular ones being SOCIAL MEDIA, BLOGS, YOUTUBE videos, etc. Essentially, these are means to let your customers know about updates from your business, like when a new product is expected. As time passes and more people come to know the calibre of your work, each of these strategies will increase your authority. It's a snowball effect: you start with a little Instagram profile and share interesting stuff there, and eventually, one of your videos goes viral, making you a household name in the industry.

I'll do your blog, I promise. Your blog is The only platform where current and potential clients may hear you speak honestly and freely. Upload a photo to your blog. Discuss about your life. While it's unnecessary to share every detail about yourself, blogging allows readers to get a sense of who you are and helps them relate to you far more deeply. People will be more receptive to your words when speaking authoritatively because emotion often wins the brain. Naturally, I should note that poor writing or factual inaccuracies can erode authority once more. Consider your content carefully before publishing it since the last thing you want is for a news or YouTube channel to feature your business! The internet may be both a boon and a burden, depending on how it is used.

Alright, let's get started. Name some individuals in your life that you regard as authoritative figures: your teacher, mentor, parents, friends, or anyone else you like. Consider why you regard them as an authority. Knowledge, experience, wisdom, and that innate sense of knowing what to do and what not to do are most likely contributing factors. The same concepts apply to Internet marketing; you must employ other instruments to accomplish the same objectives.

Keep in mind that developing your authority takes time and work. If you are here looking for a quick money plan, I can assure you that it will fail most of the time. Additionally, remember that everybody hoping to succeed and make millions of dollars has access to the Internet. Even if many businesses offer a quick fix for building authority, word-of-mouth marketing and advertising the "old-fashioned way" is still the best approach. If all you are delivering is the same garbage the rest of the market is selling and you are not adding value, stop and realise that VALUE = PROFIT. Instead, you need to establish a reputation for producing reliable, persistent material, and of the highest calibre that truly benefits people.

Learning Effective Time Management Techniques

The Eisenhower Box: Vital versus Necessary

A useful tool for making decisions, the Eisenhower Box, often called the Eisenhower Matrix, assists people in ranking tasks according to their significance and urgency. The 34th President of the United States, Dwight D. Eisenhower, renowned for his extraordinary time management abilities and capacity to concentrate on what mattered, popularized it. Tasks are grouped into four quadrants by the matrix according to two primary dimensions: importance and urgency.

Crucial and Timely (Quadrant I: Take Action First):

The tasks in this quadrant are vital to your objectives or general well-being and call for quick attention. These are frequently urgent or deadline-driven chores that require your quick attention. Taking immediate action is critical to avoid bad outcomes or take advantage of pressing possibilities.

Tasks in Quadrant II: Schedule, "Important but Not Urgent," are essential to your long-term objectives, personal development, and general success. Since they are not urgent, they are frequently neglected in favour of more important issues. But concentrating on these duties is necessary for proactive planning, smart thinking, and averting future emergencies. More time spent in this quadrant is emphasized by effective time management.

Essential, but Not Important (Quadrant III: Delegate or Limit): Although the tasks in this quadrant are time-sensitive or seem essential to others, they don't directly advance your priorities or goals. These could include unneeded meetings, disruptions, or jobs that should be reduced or assigned to save time for more important ones.

Not Critical and Not Urgent (Quadrant IV: Discard):

In the big picture, tasks in this quadrant are neither urgent nor significant. They are distractions and time wasters that don't advance your goals or add much value. To maximize productivity, it is desirable to reduce or eliminate certain tasks.

By using the Eisenhower Box, we can better decide how to spend our time and energy by visualizing the most and least essential tasks. To keep important but non-urgent tasks from becoming urgent (Quadrant I), it promotes focusing on them (Quadrant II). Long-term success depends on this strategy since it makes sure that important time and effort are spent on things that support one's objectives and vision.

Setting Priorities Methods for Reaching Maximum Productivity

The compass that helps us navigate the maze of chores and responsibilities with clarity and purpose is provided by prioritization approaches. The ABCDE approach is one effective strategy in which 'A' stands for the most critical activities, 'B' for important but less urgent chores, 'C' for nice-to-do tasks, 'D' for jobs that can be assigned, and 'E' for tasks to eliminate. By sorting jobs according to importance, this approach ensures that the most important ones are completed first. Priorities are refined using a different strategy called the Moscow method (Must have, Should have, Could have, Won't have). Tasks marked as "must have" are non-negotiable, "should have" are significant but deferable, "could have" are desirable but not necessary, and "won't have" are ones that need to be thought through further. By applying these strategies, work can be organized based on how it affects deadlines and goals, promoting a systematic approach to productivity.

Additionally, evaluating each task's worth and the effort necessary to execute it is part of the useful worth vs. Effort analysis technique. Tasmaximizeprovides great value for comparatively little work and is prioritized to maximize. These methods enable people to distinguish between what is important and what may appear urgent but is not as important. People can create a daily schedule that maximizes productivity, concentrates on high-impact tasks, and eventually moves them closer to their objectives by using these prioritizing techniques.

establishing reasonable objectives

Setting aside your feelings and views, not every aim can be accomplished. The skill of setting realistic objectives is to create a path to success by connecting our desires with real-world results. Making your goals SMART (specific, measurable, attainable, relevant, and time-bound) is a good place to start when starting this journey. Being specific helps you avoid being vague by clearly focusing on your aim. Setting and meeting a realistic goal helps you monitor your development and gives you concrete proof of your achievements. Achievability guarantees that your objective is feasible given your existing situation and aligned with your resources and skills. Time-bound goals establish a deadline, which creates a sense of urgency and dedication, while relevant goals guarantee that your goal is significant and relevant to your overall aims.

Additionally, take into account both your short- and long-term objectives. Divide long-term objectives into more achievable, smaller benchmarks. By breaking down the procedure into manageable steps and rewarding yourself when you reach each one, this method helps you get closer to your final objective. Think about your advantages and disadvantages as well. Use your advantages to achieve your goals while focusing on your disadvantages. Recall that a realistic goal should inspire and drive you rather than discourage or overwhelm you; it should be challenging but not impossible. Reaffirm that you can accomplish your goals by celebrating your small victories along the way. Essentially, achieving realistic objectives requires a combination of self-awareness, strategic planning, and the motivation to transform your aspirations into Effective Task and Time Administration

- Pomodoro Technique and Time Blocking

Two effective techniques that help with time management, productivity, and attention in the face of a hectic day are the Pomodoro Technique and Time Blocking.

Setting aside certain blocks of time for particular tasks or activities is known as time blocking. It's similar to setting up compartments in your day where you set out designated times to concentrate on different projects. For example, you may set off the first two hours of the morning for important project tasks, devote an hour to emails and other correspondence, and finally set up a meeting time. You protect yourself from multitasking and repeated distractions by doing this. Time blocking maximizes productivity by enabling intense focus and complete attention to the subject. Additionally, it gives your day structure and discipline and guarantees you prioritize important tasks.

However, Francesco Cirillo created the Pomodoro Technique, a time management technique. It divides your work into short bursts, usually 25 minutes for concentrated labour (a "Pomodoro") and 5 minutes for rest. After each Pomodoro four times, take a longer pause (approximately 15 to 30 minutes). The secret is to focus intently on your job during each Pomodoro, avoiding interruptions and diversions. This method uses the brain's short-term capacity for concentration, and the frequent pauses support mental flexibility and guard against burnout. It's a useful tool for time management and productivity gains, particularly for projects that could otherwise seem difficult or overwhelming.

Combining the two methods can work quite well. You can set out certain time slots for concentrated work using time blocking and the Pomodoro Technique to get the most out of each minute of that time. For example, you may schedule time in your morning to work on projects and utilize the Putilize Technique to divide your work into 25-minute concentrated bursts interspersed with brief breaks. This combo makes the most of your time, sharpens your focus, guarantees you do your chores on time, and preserves a good work-rest balance.

Overview

You are now headed toward financial independence. You are aware that the path won't be simple. Financial independence is attained via diligent work and smart planning, just like anything else. Baby steps and constancy are the first things to do. You have the correct mindset to keep going until you reach your goal after you decide to follow this path. The path to financial freedom consists of five steps, each of which may require several steps.

Planning, or the preliminary evaluation of what you have, what needs to be done, and how to get there, is the first step. Just keep in mind that the planning process will vary as you proceed down this road, so view your plans as flexible documents that will expand and contract as necessary.

Preserving the original emergency money is the second stage. Putting this in place before you even begin to address the bills is essential for your overall health.

Paying off debts is the third phase. Based on your training, abilities, and skills, it is up to you how you accomplish this. To achieve these goals, pay attention and discover how to boost your income, as numerous avenues are available.

The long-term planning phase is the fourth step. Thinking about your goals for the next five, ten, or even fifteen years is important. You must be ready for these changes as your children grow and evolve and your family's dynamics shift.

Knowing that your retirement years are secured is the last step toward achieving financial freedom. By following the instructions and embarking on this adventure, this is achieved. While it could take some trial and error, consistency is key to maintaining the objectives.

First to Fifth Tip #1: Realism

Recognizing and recognizing the financial situation is the first step towards being financially independent. Take some time to list everything you must pay each month, including recurrent expenses like debt repayment and utilities. Putting things down on paper makes it easier to see what you'll have to deal with moving forward.

2. Extended Objectives and Schemes

The next stage is to develop your financial objectives and strategies for achieving financial independence. Paying off debt and listing your desired outcomes, like opening a savings account or purchasing a car with cash, should be part of your goals. The plan must include information about your debts, monthly payment amounts, and anticipated payoff date.

3. What Is Your Self-Concept?

We are what we think. What is your opinion about yourself? Do you consider yourself to be financially independent? Or do you consider yourself to be financially strained and constrained by debt? To get from where you are to where you want to be, you must change how you think. It all begins with an idea.

4. Incorporate Your Partner or Spouse

It makes sense to involve your roommate in your efforts to achieve financial independence if you share financial responsibilities and live together. Have a discussion, sit down, and involve them in creating the lists, creating the plans, and establishing the objectives. Let them serve as your guarantors and make mutual commitments to persevere.

5. Get an Education. Learning something new occasionally is a necessary step toward financial independence. You can take any financial tutorials and classes to assist you in achieving your financial objectives. Putting money and effort into improving your financial management skills makes sense. This will give

you a new perspective on your finances and income, which will assist you overcome financial obstacles.

What makes you poor or broke?

Approximately 8% of the global

Many people in the population are impoverished, but why?

I'll give you the low-income explanations for most people. And if you want to overcome poverty, you need to stay away from these money mistakes.

They Lack Specified

Budgetary Objectives

Every financial move you take starts with a set of financial objectives. Put differently, you are shaping your future financial decisions when you set financial goals.

They provide you with a sense of purpose and financial direction. Furthermore, without them, there would be no accountability in your financial life.

For instance, if you wish to save $10,000 this year, you must consider all your spending options.

Periodically in opposition to the following query:

"Will this help or hinder my efforts to save $10,000?" A simple question like that might be the difference between living frugally and making impulsive purchases. I would even venture to suggest that seemingly insignificant details could distinguish between wealth or bankruptcy.

A Few Quick Tips for Financial Goal Setting

Setting financial goals should be your first step to avoid becoming broke. At the very least, I recommend setting two habit goals and two success targets. If you're unfamiliar with them, allow me to clarify.

Goals with a conclusion are called achievement objectives. They almost always have something to do with a specific monetary amount in personal finance. Whether you aim to save $10,000 (as in our example), pay off all of your debt, or save for a down payment on a house, all goals have an endpoint or the moment you know you've succeeded.

Conversely, habit targets lack a definite endpoint. Since they are ongoing, consistency is the goal. Investing a certain percentage of your income each time you get paid—not less than ten, but perhaps more—is a great illustration of a behavioural goal.

I will now admit that habit goals are harder to maintain than accomplishment goals since they are less exciting. Therefore, I implore you to pair them with a goal for success.

If your accomplishment goal is to invest $10,000 in Forex this year, for instance, you may pair it with a habit goal to save at least

20% of your income each time you receive your paycheck. Although the habit goal is ongoing, it will help you achieve your accomplishment goal more.

Excellent illustrations of financial aspirations for success:

● Have enough money saved up to cover your the following car.

Eliminate debt from credit cards:

● Finish the mortgage.

● Put up enough cash for a six-month trip.

● Give to God, and then invest each time you receive a paycheck—at least 10% of your salary, excluding retirement.

● Every quarter, read at least one book about personal finance.

● Record your purchases in your spending diary each evening.

● Schedule a weekly financial meeting with your partner, financial counsellor, or yourself. Their budget is nonexistent.

Most people are broke primarily because they don't follow a budget. In recent studies conducted by the U.S. Bank, only 41% of Americans follow their spending plan. Furthermore, how do you know when you are deviating from your financial plan if you don't have a budget?

Making a budget enables you to organize, track, and assess your spending habits. Your path to achieving your financial goals is marked.

They Don't Monitor Their Expenses

The majority of people are broke in part because they don't keep track of their expenses. However, it disproves the budget concept itself. Money might easily escape your grasp if you don't monitor your expenditures. Before you know it, though, you're broke and don't even understand why.

I like to compare keeping an eye on your spending to being a parent. Given that young children tend to wander out, what should a parent do? Observe them.

That also holds for your finances. If you don't closely monitor your spending habits, money has a way of fading away. You must monitor your spending, whether it's at restaurants, grocery stores, or retail establishments.

If not, you would start to wonder what happened to your money.

Exercise 4: Track Your Spending and Form Mindful Habits

You have arranged your debts according to importance and devised a plan to settle them. You need to know where your money is going before you try to figure out how to make it cover everything. Seeing where your money goes differs from merely glancing at your revenue and expenses on paper. Budgets and money management systems are not broken by large expenses but rather by small ones. You will need to monitor where every last penny goes for at least a month (preferably, you will be tracking in some capacity moving forward). You must pinpoint the areas of your wallet where careless spending has left a hole.

FIRST STEP:

Take a notepad in your pocket and fasten the cover with a paperclip. If you are unable to list a purchase when it is finished, the paperclip will be used to store your daily receipts.

Step 2:

You will note every item you make no matter how big or little you buy.

Step 3:

You will review your daily list of purchases at the end of the day and reconcile receipts that were not entered. Add up all of your purchases.

Step Four:

To get the overall daily spending, add the other costs incurred during the day, such as bills paid.

Step Five:

You will add up your daily expenses to generate a weekly total at the end of each week. Compare it to the weekly revenue you made.

Step 6:

Look over your spending to identify any instances of "mindless" purchases. Determine which goods can be decreased or perhaps deleted. Note any areas where you are prone to weakness or the desire to spend carelessly. This will assist you in avoiding such circumstances and temptations.

Section Two

How is a budget balanced?

I

A congressional act is not necessary to balance your pricing range. You need someone committed to reaching their financial objectives, has the self-control to stick to your plan, and is prepared to make the necessary changes.

These are five different methods.

1. Create a budget.

Examine your financial records before creating a price range. Credit card and bank statements can be used to determine how much money you make and how much you typically spend on costs. Divide the financial information into two categories: anticipated expenses and anticipated revenue.

Wages, earnings from self-employment, earnings from investments, and earnings from other sources must all be included in the predicted earnings. Next, include anticipated costs such as electricity, cable and phone bills, and mortgage or rent.

Lastly, deduct anticipated fees from expected profits to get the amount left over after fees are paid. The remaining amount must be saved for rainy days, utilized to settle debt, or allocated to other financial goals.

2. Distinguish the needs from the wants.

Additionally, divide your anticipated costs into two categories: nondiscretionary and discretionary charges. Expenses that fall under the category of "wishes" include entertainment, dining out, and fitness centre memberships. Rent, utilities, groceries, and nondiscretionary payments are needed.

Consider discretionary costs to see if you can identify costs that would be reduced or eliminated.

3. Adjust your expenses

Changing your finances regularly will show the true expenses for each area. Compare actual spending to budgeted amounts.

Use phone budgeting apps if you're tech-savvy to help you keep track of expenses. Alternatively, if you enjoy keeping records the old-fashioned way, keep a notepad handy to record your spending.

4. overview and routinely regulate

Prepare a finance plan every month or at the beginning of each pay period. This allows you to review your finances from the previous month and pinpoint areas where you wish to cut back on spending. Make any necessary changes to assist you in achieving your financial goals, such as debt reduction or savings.

5. The means to enjoy life's pleasures

Remember to schedule in time for some indulgences, such as date evenings or a new outfit or pair of shoes. Making arrangements in advance will help you understand what you might be able to afford and also acts as a reminder to take care of yourself occasionally.

Establish financial equilibrium

Your finances can assist you:

Keep a record of your earnings and expenses.

Keep up with your monthly expenses.

Prepare for unforeseen expenses.

Avoid going overboard with your purchases.

Decide how much you want to spend shopping to satisfy your financial needs.

A budget consists of five parts.

The amount of money you need to work with monthly is your profits after taxes. Your earnings may also differ if you work for yourself, are a seasonal or part-time employee, or receive payment for using a service. Take your annual wages and divide by 12 to get your monthly pricing range. Make use of this sum as your monthly earnings.

Monthly fixed prices: These expenses typically remain the same, or nearly the same, from month to month. They are made up of payments for fixed mortgage repayments, cable, internet, utilities, and your hire or loan.

Monthly changes in costs are known as variable costs. They include groceries, gas, daily coffee, eating out, and entertainment costs.

Expenses that arise occasionally include clothing, gifts, and holidays.

Savings: Allocate funds in your budget for immediate emergency needs and longer-term investments to advance your financial objectives.

Your pay may also vary if you work for yourself, are self-employed, are a seasonal or part-time worker, or are paid with a fee. Take your annual earnings and divide by 12 to create your monthly budget. This sum will serve as your monthly income.

Sort through your variable costs.

Make an initial budget using reasonable expectations. Adjust your expenditures for the next few months after that. Keep track of all your receipts for your purchases; record them in a notebook or make a spreadsheet. Move backwards for your budget and make any necessary adjustments after monitoring your expenditures for a few months.

Be prepared for sporadic costs.

Make space in your budget for unforeseen expenses such as clothes, accessories, and trips. Find out more about budgeting for one-time expenses.

Budgets are also for saving.

Make financial savings a part of your budget by paying yourself first. Once your paycheck is deposited, arrange to have this amount transferred to a savings account. Shopping becomes less complicated as you automate it.

Section Two

Changes from Fortune

Most people now doubt that anything in the history of the economy has ever gone so quickly or had such an impact as the Information Revolution. However, the Industrial Revolution was advancing more slowly during the same period and likely impacted what would happen if no one had.

-Printer Peter

My childhood was troubled like most childhoods are. But now I realize how fortunate I was to have had a good education overall. One of my earliest souvenirs is the trip I took to live in New York City for a year with my mother, who was getting an excellent education in early childhood education. A five-year-old boy from North Carolina once told me that his skating lessons at the Rockefeller Center's indoor rink were an amazing experience. A smile never disappears from the memory of eating hot chestnuts purchased from street vendors in the bitter cold after lunch. When we got home, my father said I sounded like the only little Yankee. Never did I completely recover a single Southern accent. I see my mixed-language speaking as a reflection of my exceptional good fortune.

Goodbye. Both of them came from my nation and achieved great success in their lives. I understood that their achievement was based on the spiritual and internal economic basis that my grandparents had laid. My mother's parents were both college graduates, which was unusual for African Americans in the first part of the 20th century. Reba Hoffman, my grandma, was a librarian and spoke French well. My grandfather, Guy was the principal of a high school, the proprietor of a. Ford Model T and a home on forty-one acres. They belonged to Tennessee and were respectable members of the expanding middle class. Reba used to make and mend clothes with his Singer sewing machine, a common tool for small enterprises covered later in this chapter. My grandparents hired help to handle your farms and lands while they farmed and reared pigs and hens together. They believed that any pattern made them wealthy. As African Americans living in the South in the 1930s, they were the only ones who felt safe.

Many people at the time, particularly Black people, could hardly afford to fill.

The gas tank of their car. What if you could provide enough money to buy just one car? He had other matters to attend to before that. Nevertheless, here's a family tale that was relayed by a friend who, while refuelling in the city as a teenager, related the story of how my grandfather stopped at a gas station in his Model T, and the young cashier asked Principal Hoffman how much petrol he wanted in the tank. Subsequently, my grandfather inquired about the tank's capacity. As soon as he heard back, "About 10 gallons," he exclaimed, "Well fill it up boy! Fill it!" The anecdote made us laugh a lot but also conveyed that my grandfather was an affluent guy.

Nevertheless, if the Hoffman family from the 1930s were part of the average suburban middle-class home today, we could experience something akin to shivering. They are so powerful that I think they even made it to a modest palace owned by the wealthy. The house has central heating and air conditioning, a washing machine and dryer, a refrigerator, a freezer, a dishwasher, TVs, computers, microwave ovens, and even self-sprinklers. To describe even a few of these appliances is to indicate extraordinary wealth.

The difference in quality of life between my grandmother and grandfather and the lives of many Americans now highlights an intriguing phenomenon: our concept of wealth is ever-evolving. This holds for all cultures worldwide, not just the United States. A lifestyle like this, which we now consider practically a birthright for Americans in the twenty-first century, was unimaginable to a nineteenth-century Earth baron.

We can also reasonably forecast which indoor items that we now consider Lux will become typical installations tomorrow. As an illustration, most families in the 1950s desired a single TV in the bedroom when I was a little boy. TVs are commonplace in today's homes, often found in the kitchen, family bedroom, and most bedrooms in a single residence. However, "home theater," formerly considered a luxury owned by wealthy individuals such as Hollywood moguls, has become nearly standard in suburban America.

flexibility in the meaning of fortune for the two of us as individuals in this one society

It demonstrates how money and our hopes for its benefits are viewed through the lens of seeking. The standard by which wealth is measured is still developing. The method by which European immigrants to America amassed wealth and witnessed it drastically shift throughout the Industrial Revolution.

Inside means such as these measurements from fortune developed for some time again when the information age arrived. The common denominator, however, always stays the same: a sincere desire to live one's best life.

Options Trading: What Is It?

Trading options function similarly to exchanging another financial item. Still, you are giving customers the option to purchase that financial instrument rather than buying or selling a genuine financial product.

You should manage specific financial decisions meant to be made and exchanged when you engage in choice-exchanging. Options trading will not function on certain markets, including Forex, since these markets are not designed to handle the contractual side of the deal.

You will need to think about two directions when you begin trading options: buying and selling options.

When you buy a choice, you are buying the option to buy the hidden resource that the choice you have chosen to buy addresses. You have two options: you can decidedecide to buy stocks when they are increasing (bullish) or dropping (negative). As long as you are trading by the proper process to help you profit from the agreement's inherent value, you can profit financially from either of these purchasing strategies.

There will be two purchases that you must make. Thus, you must pay close attention to the lapse date when picking. The initial purchase will initiate the acquisition of the actual options, providing you with sufficient means to choose to purchase the fundamental resource at a predetermined cost.

The next purchase will be made assuming that you exercise that right; in that event, you should exercise your decision to purchase the fundamental resource at the price specified earlier. Should you decide to buy, you must purchase the expiration date; otherwise, your option will become worthless, and you won't be able to benefit from it. ccc

When you are selling choices, you can sell to a rising (bullish) or sinking (negative) market. Again, the one you choose will depend on the technique you use to generate profits from your trades. Later on, we will talk more about the two techniques related to swapping choices, called call and put choices.

In the meantime, realize that you are responsible for creating the contract under which any options you sell will be sold. This suggests that to make your decision, you should decide on the strike price and termination date you want to join in your agreement. IfIf the agreement buyer chooses to exercise their right to purchase the stocks you have available for purchase with your contracts, you will also need to complete the transaction.

What Makes Options Superior to Stocks?

Two reasons options are better than common stocks and other financial products. The fact that these particular swaps assist you against the odds is perhaps the most persuasive reason people enjoy exchanging selections. The biggest risk you run when exchanging choices is that your option ends up being worthless, in which case you are just out of pocket for the cost of the choice agreement. Even if this setback still affects your main issue, it is guaranteed bad luck, unlike in the stock exchange, where bad luck might be sudden and severe.

The fact that choices are the least expensive currency to purchase and exchange contributes to their popularity. The cost to initiate exchanges is substantially less than that of some other financial instruments now on the market. You are not exchanging a complete resource but rather an agreement addressing the entire resource.

Lastly, overseeing specialized research for a decision is far simpler than overseeing specialized research for oil stocks.

When conducting a specialist analysis of crude stocks, you should concentrate on particular fundamentals that inform you about whether the stock is worth investing in. When it comes to choices, the important things are less important, and you may rely even more only on patterns and the overall likelihood of how that particular decision will behave. Preparing for a swap of selections is far less laborious and still provides remarkable accuracy that yields significant profits.

CONFLICT

The most common problem people have when handling money is not so much about obtaining it as it is about holding onto the money they have, regardless of how simple or complex the process is to obtain it. Don't get me wrong; obtaining Money can be challenging, but maintaining Money is easier for most people—including you—than obtaining it.

Even if it's not particularly common, almost everyone up to the age of managing Money has a way of receiving it. Over the years, I've seen that people's biggest problem is figuring out how to hold onto the Money they've genuinely worked so hard to earn. It's funny, but in my experience, it's easier to generate Money than to hold onto it. But that's the reality.

I could provide countless examples of individuals about the above, but I want to be honest so that everything I write will be relevant. Whenever you decide to start saving your Money, you notice how hard it has been for you—it feels like you're in jail. Observe what transpires when you start thinking, "Is it not my money?" Suddenly, you find yourself going on a spending binge.

You only give up when the Money runs out. It's actually at that stage that you start to become financially sane. The pitiful thing about spending is that, as you're spending, you cease to recognise the work you put into creating the things you're spending so easily. Money spent is not always a bad thing—overspending is!

The diligent worker
Allow me to lead you down memory lane. Consider how difficult it was for you to obtain a cent. While some people receive their Money every day, you might receive it once a month.

Consider the hours you worked to earn your salary. You might even be underpaid in this case. Consider the strain you endure working for a paycheck for at least 25 days per month.

Remember the restless evenings you spent ensuring everything was ready for work the following day? Or perhaps more accurately, how do you continue to think about work even as you sleep? Remember the strange times you had to wake up for work? Do you need me to remind you of your work pressure, particularly from your boss? Do I need to mention it again? Time will not allow me to do it, though.

To highlight to you the extent of your tireless work ethic, I outlined some of the hardships you endure to receive a paycheck. I know you frequently overlook these factors before overspending with your earnings.

If you took the time to think these things through, the knowledge alone may force you to stop overspending, but you probably forgot about them as soon as you earned your paycheck. Pain can change your perspective, but it's possible that you haven't had enough yet.

While spending is necessary, using up all of your Money is not. Why is your income not commensurate with your labour if you put in so much effort? Nobody is more puzzled than the person who, after foolishly spending his previous month's salary, has to start over financially every month.

Do you enjoy the hardships you endure to make Money? Your financial management style will undoubtedly provide you with an answer to it. Many people have to start over financially before they receive their next salary; will you be one of them, or will you insist on changing things?

I'm sure you must have tried a lot of different strategies to keep your money, but they have all failed.